ABSOLUTE BEGINNER BUSINESS KIT & ONLINE MARKETING FOR THE YOUNG CEO

DANNY DIN

INTRODUCTION

Running a business may not make you rich. In fact, you might easily become rich as an employee than as a business owner.

No, I'm not bearing bad news. The facts agree: one in five businesses fail within the first year, five in ten businesses within the first five years, and only one in four businesses make it to year 15 (Investopedia). Given these numbers, we can argue that you don't have to lead the next startup or fast-growing e-commerce store. The chances of success aren't as high as you dreamed.

The good news is, no one is born business savvy. The better news is, you can build a business at a young age. Mark Zuckerberg co-founded Facebook (now Meta) at 19 with no prior business experience (and a ton of programming experience, nevertheless). Hillary Yip began her learning startup,

MinorMynas at 10, and twenty-year-old Moziah Bridges launched Mo's Bows at age nine with the help of his mother. You're not too young to start, stay, and soar.

The best news is, this book is your go-to toolbox for building a successful e-commerce outfit as a young entrepreneur. Like every other toolbox, the book offers you multiple tools across several chapters, including:

- Daring to be innovative as a young CEO, with references to high-performing individuals who are modelling the entrepreneurship journey.
- How to leverage social marketing for building your e-commerce store. What numbers should you monitor, and why do you need the numbers? We explore the fundamental blueprints for selling anything online.
- How to brainstorm product ideas. Morgan Newman and Casey Elsass, founders of MixedMatch (now Bushwick Kitchen), show that you can easily turn the mundane into the extraordinary and make some money while at it (proved by a $100k+ profit in their first ten months).
- Why your audience matters and how to find the people for your business. On most days, building your target audience is like finding a pack of evasive pins from a haystack. You don't have to

stress out. Our list of thoughtful questions included in this book will help you figure out your target market in no time.

- Selling like crazy, and understanding how to optimize proven sale funnels for converting potential users to quick-paying customers. Together, we explore the Moz funnel for generating sales leads and taking your leads through the conversion process.

- Launching your store and avoiding the trap that many young entrepreneurs fall into while at it. This chapter covers the essential stuff on creating a brand name, planning your logistics ahead, alternatives for creating an e-commerce website, and more.

Entrepreneurship, in three words, is "learn, then do". Thus, each chapter in **Young CEOs: Absolute Business Starter Kit** includes a "Work it Out" section for converting the lessons into practicable steps.

This book will not give you your first huge payout. Instead, it will equip you with all the technical need-to-know, the entire thingamabob, and have you ready to launch when the light goes green. So, are you ready? Let's dive in!

GENERATION NEXT: BOLD STRATEGIES OF YOUNG CEOS REDEFINING THE FUTURE OF BUSINESS

AS A YOUNG CEO, being daring and innovative is key to achieving success and making a significant impact in your industry. Regardless of the industry, it takes courage to step out of the traditional ways of doing things and push the boundaries of what is feasible. In today's rapidly evolving business landscape, you need a lot of guts to stay ahead of the competition and meet the ever-changing needs of consumers.

The world is changing rapidly, and so is the business world. Advancements in fields such as Artificial Intelligence and Web3 have shown that it is possible to push the limits of growth and development.

Since the turn of the century, we have seen a surge of young entrepreneurs stepping into the business world, taking up leadership roles and changing how businesses operate. These young CEOs are innovative, creative, and unafraid to take risks. Leaning on a plethora of knowledge, and boundless access to technological and human resources, these young entrepreneurs have carved trails for those coming behind. Beyond this, they are creating blueprints for selling to audiences with a short attention span.

In this chapter, we consider the stories of three entrepreneurs who have made a mark through successful online businesses, and the lessons we can learn from them.

Evan Spiegel:

Evan Spiegel is the co-founder and CEO of Snapchat, a social media platform that allows users to send transient photos and videos. Spiegel founded Snapchat in 2011 while he was still a student at Stanford University. Working with two other co-founders, Spiegel aimed to build an app that encouraged sharing multimedia files that captured a range of human emotions. Communication between users didn't have to be picture-perfect if it was genuine.

While social media apps like Instagram and Facebook allowed users to upload files and tag others, Snapchat's functionality encouraged users to relate as they were without the pressure of "branding" their social media presence.

Today, Snapchat has over 265 million daily active users, and it has become one of the most popular social media platforms among young people. The selling point of Snapchat? Snaps. Spiegel identified the insatiable need for an audience to communicate with friends and family and led the development team to introduce auxiliary features such as *Story,* *Snapcash,* and *Snapcode.*

Lessons to learn

Spiegel's entrepreneurial growth results from his ability to create a product that meets the needs of his target audience. A 2014 research led by the team at the University of Washington identified the Generation Z group as Snapchat's core user group. Knowing that young people want a social media platform for sharing content that disappears quickly, Spiegel structured the company's mission to reflect this.

If you run an online business, identifying your target audience is pivotal to launching a successful outfit. However, ask:

- What makes my target audience unique?
- What are the primary needs of my target audience?
- Does my product solve any of these needs? How?

These questions will guide your short-term and long-term approaches as you build your business. You would determine if your product eases users' work or compounds their worries. As with Patrick Collison, who co-founded Stripe, this will influence the steps you adopt to create a versatile product.

John and Patrick Collison:

The idea for Stripe came to Patrick because he was frustrated with the difficulty of accepting payments online for a previous business venture. He realised a need for a simple and easy-to-use payment processing system to integrate with any website and handle any online bill.

Working with his younger brother John, a self-taught programmer from the early age of eight, they co-founded Stripe in 2010, having dropped out of MIT and Harvard, respectively to focus on building the product. Before co-creating the financial venture designed to be the next PayPal, the brothers had sold a business, Auctomatic, a move that elevated their status to millionaires. Patrick attributed the successful sale of Auctomatic to his exceptional performance at the Young Scientists and Technology Exhibition a few years earlier.

But building a successful online business takes more than smartness or programming knowledge. The brothers figured that Stripe could declutter the complex payment process on the internet. Online payments could be as simple as embedding a video link.

Was this idea successful? Absolutely. It was so persuasive that Elon Musk, who founded PayPal, threw in a lump investment sum.

Today, Stripe has become one of the world's most successful payment processing companies, processing billions of dollars in transactions yearly.

Lesson on Starting

The Collisons' success stems from their ability to recognise the need for a payment processing system that was easy to use and accessible to businesses of all sizes.

All thriving products or businesses share a common understanding: you find a specific need, and match your product's objective to meet this need. As with Brian Cheeky, it doesn't matter if you're in fintech, entertainment, consumer goods, or hospitality.

Brian Chesky:

You may not know Brian, but you know his product - Airbnb, the famous company that allows people to rent out their homes or apartments to travellers. Chesky started the company in 2008, with over 4 million listings in over 220 countries.

The idea for Airbnb came about when Chesky and Gebbia, his roommate, struggled to pay their rent. They decided to rent air mattresses in their living room to people attending a design conference in San Francisco. They created a simple website to advertise their "Air Bed and Breakfast" and were surprised by the level of interest they received.

Realising they had stumbled upon a business idea, Chesky and Gebbia teamed up with their former roommate, Nathan Blecharczyk, to create Airbnb (**innovation**). The platform launched in 2009 and quickly attracted millions of users worldwide.

Brian's entrepreneurial prowess is seen in his risk-taking,

such as expanding into new geographical markets and offering unique experiences to guests.

Lessons to learn

Chesky's success results from his ability to create a product (home letting) that meets a need (guest-lodging). He understood that travellers wanted a more authentic and affordable experience. Airbnb meets that need.

Working It Out:

1. What's your primary motivation for running a business?

2. Itemise three words that define your business. The words should capture the identified gap, the specific solution you offer, and the differentiating factor, respectively (for instance, Stripe's three words would be *payment*, *seamless*, and *integration*).

3. Would you still run your business if you didn't make profits for three months? Yes / No. Why?

2

CRACK THE E-COMMERCE CODE: THE ART OF VIRAL SOCIAL MARKETING

WHEN YOUNG ENTREPRENEURS consider setting up an online business, they imagine their product as the next Snapchat, Amazon, or Alibaba. Being ambitious isn't wrong, however, the noble goal of every e-commerce establishment is to make money by identifying a target audience's needs and creating a product that meets that need.

Consider your favorite online stores. Top dropshipping outfits such as Doba and Salehoo simplify online shopping for users in bulk or units. DoorDash and Uber Eats make food delivery as easy as sending an email. Email marketing platforms like MailChimp and Mailerlite offer a range of products and features suitable for businesses as well as individuals. These six companies - and many others - stay afloat because they solve a specific problem and make a ton of profit while at it.

Social selling has emerged as a key strategy for e-commerce and online marketing. It involves using social media platforms to engage with potential customers, build relationships, and ultimately convert them into paying customers. From this, we can deduce a practicable equation for running a successful e-commerce store, regardless of location or niche.

E-commerce = Social Media Platform + Customer Relationships + Sales.

Image source: Trootech.

No e-commerce business succeeds without a vibrant social media presence. Don't just think about Instagram. TikTok, email campaign lists, Facebook pages, Twitter communities and spaces, are other ways businesses can consolidate a social media presence in an ever-noisy online world.

How about customer relationships? Customer relationships follow a loop that begins with potential users. If you've ever skipped a Wix ad on YouTube, you escaped the loop that converts potential users to paying clients. When you launch a product, thousands of humans are most likely to want the product. That group is your target audience or market, and the numbers can go as far as one million, depending on your offerings.

You may ask, "Why am I not recording sales in millions?" It's because the humans in your target audience do not all become customers. Some users exit the loop at the end of a free trial. Some after three months, when they spot a typo in your email campaign, or if they experience a five-second lag while completing an order on your website. The **customers** are those who stay, who, through active interactions with your product, build a trustworthy relationship. They are the ones who drive recorded **sales**.

The Blueprint for a Successful E-commerce Outfit

Having identified a unique problem that your product solves, three factors determine the success of the e-commerce business you build around this product: social media awareness, customers, and sales. Given these factors, any e-commerce business that outshines competitors:

Build a Strong Social Media Presence

One of the first steps in online marketing is building a strong social media presence. This involves creating profiles on social media platforms like Facebook, Instagram, Twitter, and LinkedIn. Ensure that the brand's messaging, visuals, and branding are consistent across all platforms, as this builds credibility and shows competence. A consistent brand image also ensures the brand is easily recognizable across all channels.

Young entrepreneurs often worry about the predictability of social media branding. Won't users be tired of seeing the same content on my page? The answer is no. Instead, your users trust your business because they know what to expect. The core values of excellence, accountability and credibility assure them whenever they interact with your page.

Create Engaging Content

Once a strong social media presence is established, the next step is creating engaging content. This could include blog posts, videos, infographics, or social media posts. The content should be informative, entertaining, and relevant to the audience's interests and needs. Elf Cosmetics, a top-selling cosmetic e-commerce store, leverages TikTok to create videos describing its products. They also collaborate with other TikTok users to create videos addressing their customers' questions.

By creating valuable content, your business can attract potential customers and keep them engaged with the brand.

Social Media Advertising

Social media advertising is also an important aspect of social selling. Platforms like Facebook, Instagram, and Twitter offer highly targeted advertising options, allowing businesses to reach specific demographics and interests. By using targeted advertizing, businesses can ensure that their ads are seen by the right people, increasing the chances of conversion.

Engaging Directly with Potential Customers

In addition to advertizing, businesses can use social media to engage with potential customers directly. You can respond to comments and messages, plan contests and give-aways, and offer new or long-term clients exclusive discounts. Humans love a responsive brand; you can build a loyal following and create a positive brand image by engaging your users across social media platforms.

Social Media Analytics

Social media analytics is another important tool for social selling. By tracking metrics such as engagement, click-through, and conversion rates, businesses can gain valuable insights into how their social media efforts are performing. This information can be used to optimize future campaigns and improve the overall effectiveness of social selling.

Social Selling Tools and Platforms

You can scale your e-commerce businesses even further by using tools and platforms for streamlining social media efforts. Buffer helps users schedule posts, manage multiple social media accounts from one control room, and track social media activity. With Calendly, you can conveniently plan your calendar and schedules and prevent crash meetings. Michelle Kanemitsu who runs a fashion, skincare, and vlogger brand, uses Notion to plan her social media content.

By exploring tools available for optimized productivity,

you can save time and resources while effectively managing your social media presence.

An Example of a Successful E-commerce Brand

One successful example of social selling is Glossier, a cosmetics brand that has leveraged social media to grow its business. The company has a strong presence on Instagram, showcasing user-generated content and engaging with customers through comments and direct messages. Glossier also uses targeted advertizing on Facebook and Instagram to reach potential customers and offers exclusive promotions to social media followers. With a 2022 annual revenue ranging from $100M - $250M, Glossier has built a winning business by following these steps to create a successful e-commerce brand.

Working it Out

1. Do you leverage social media for your business? How?
2. What are your top three go-to tools for increased productivity? How can you better optimize your business's productivity with these tools?
3. Do you sell on TikTok? Draw out a one-month TikTok content plan for your business, including your goals and the metrics (followers, views, comments) that would determine the success of these goals.

3

FROM THE OUTSIDE IN: WHY BASIC NEEDS CAN LEAD TO KILLER E-COMMERCE PRODUCT IDEAS

SO FAR WE have looked at two major ingredients for kickstarting a fast-growing e-commerce brand: identifying an audience's needs and using social media to create a strong online presence. A third fundamental piece is creating a feasible product idea from the need you've identified.

Entrepreneurs often become stuck in the rut of finding a brilliant product idea. It may feel like every niche or industry is saturated, and every product that can be created already exists in the market. There are at least twenty active alternatives to Airbnb and ten well-known alternatives to Instagram, so why try?

Morgan Newman and her co-founder Casey Elsass showed that sometimes you don't need to look for the extraordinary if you can make one out of your environment. Infusing pure honey with chilli flakes, they branded it as

MixedMatch, made a profit of $170,000 in ten months, and eventually rebranded the product into Bushwick Kitchen, though not without their share of challenges.

We see from their experience that an online product idea is preceded by a willingness to try something new. Young entrepreneurs ignore the fact that most human needs are basic. We don't fancy the extraordinary as much as we like to imagine.

Arguably, there are no formulas for molding a winning product idea. However, with well-detailed, specific market research, and a persuasive understanding of cashflow fundamentals for running an e-commerce outfit, you're one step closer to discovering your e-commerce gem.

MARKET RESEARCH

Market research is the process of gathering information about the market, including consumer preferences, competition, and industry trends. Market research aims to inform business decisions and strategies, ensuring that businesses can identify opportunities and make informed decisions about their products and services.

One market research strategy is gathering data through surveys and focus groups. Surveys can be conducted online, in-person, or through email, providing valuable information about consumer preferences and behavior. Focus groups, on the other hand, allow businesses to gather feedback from individuals in a more interactive setting. This feedback can provide valuable insights into consumer preferences and help businesses to refine their products and services.

Another strategy for conducting market research is to analyze existing data. This can include analyzing online search data, social media trends, and other data sources to gain insights into consumer behavior and preferences. This data can inform business decisions and strategies, helping businesses identify gaps in the market and opportunities for growth.

CASH FLOW FUNDAMENTALS

Cash flow fundamentals are the basic principles of managing cash flow in a business. Cashflow is the cumulative sum that flows into and out of a business, and it is essential for ensuring that a business is able to meet its financial obligations and make investments in growth.

One key component of making an e-commerce brand work is learning how to manage accounts receivable and accounts payable. Accounts receivable is the amount of money that is owed to a business by its customers, while accounts payable is the amount of money that a business owes to its vendors and suppliers. It is essential for businesses to manage both accounts receivable and accounts payable effectively in order to maintain a healthy cash flow.

Another component of cashflow fundamentals is forecasting and budgeting. As a young entrepreneur, you don't want just to get things done as they come. Your business should run with a defined cashflow forecast and a budget that outlines your expected cash inflows and outflows for the coming year. This can help businesses to identify potential cashflow issues and plan for them accordingly.

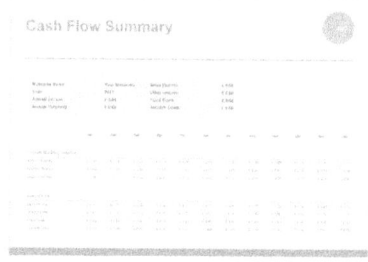

A cash flow template for an e-commerce store.

FINDING BRILLIANT PRODUCT Ideas Through Market Research

One approach to finding a brilliant product idea online is to identify trends and gaps in the market (market research). By analyzing search engine data, social media trends, and other online data sources, businesses can gain valuable insights into what consumers are looking for and what products are currently in demand. This can help businesses to identify gaps in the market that they can fill with their own unique products or services.

For example, Hims, a men's wellness company, identified a gap in the market for affordable, accessible men's health products. By analyzing online search data, the company discovered that many men were searching for information on hair loss, erectile dysfunction, and other health concerns, but were not finding the information or products they needed. Hims created a line of affordable, discreetly packaged health products that could be easily ordered online, filling a gap in the market and earning the company millions in revenue.

Another approach to finding a brilliant product idea online is to identify niche audiences. By analyzing online forums, social media groups, and other online communities, you can identify groups of consumers with specific needs or interests that are not being met by current products or services.

With this, you can identify unique product ideas that can meet the needs of these niche audiences. Beyond that though, you are assured that your product ideas will scale, having found a waiting, ready market for the products you launch from your niche-identifying.

For example, MVMT, a watch and accessories brand, identified a niche audience of young, style-conscious consumers who were looking for high-quality, affordable watches. By analyzing social media trends and online forums, the company identified a gap in the market for watches that were both stylish and affordable. MVMT created a line of watches that appealed to this niche audience, earning the company millions in revenue.

Working It Out

1. Who are the top three performing companies in your industry? Research their e-commerce marketing model and compare your findings.

2. If you run an online business, do you track your cash inflow and outflow? What three tools can you use to improve your cashflow knowledge??

4

REACH FOR THE STARS: LAUNCHING A DIGITAL STORE OR BUSINESS

LET'S talk about selling - the actual stuff, the dig-your-hands-in-the-dirt aspect of entrepreneurship. If we assume that at the time of starting out, every young entrepreneur is at point A, with the hope of arriving at point Z, when the digital store is launched. How do you move from A to Z without wanting to quit midway? How do you overcome the overwhelming feeling of being an e-commerce boss?

Idea discovery is a crucial first step to any winning digital store, but it's only the first step. Think of running an e-commerce store as a marathon; finding a product idea is the initial hurdle you cross to garner momentum for the rest of the journey. You have to test your idea with potential customers (through surveys, free samples, etc), partner with a manufacturer or supplier, create and optimize your e-commerce website, and plan shipping and delivery, amongst other things—young entrepreneurs with these capacities transition from potential storeowners to actual e-commerce bosses.

If you're starting your e-commerce store from scratch, here's a brief summary of the key steps to make your business dreams a reality:

- Validate your product idea.
- Find a manufacturer or supplier.
- Create a brand name or identity.
- Create your e-commerce website or selling channels.
- Build a social media presence.
- Prepare your shipping and delivery strategy.
- Cover your marketing ends.

(Task: What step(s) would you add to or remove from this list? Why do you consider the step(s) necessary for addition or removal?)

Validate Your Product Idea.

Idea validation boosts your chances of business success. While validating your idea, you spot potential weaknesses and figure out what you can do to beat competitors (if your idea already exists) or position yourself as an authority.

One of the easiest ways to do this is to talk to people. Gather a composite sample of people who fit your target audience and share your idea over coffee. In your conversations, ask how much they would be willing to exchange for a solution that meets their needs. Talk less about your product or business, and more about the challenge facing them.

Image source: Digital Natives.

For instance, if you want to sell personalized sporting apparel for high school teams, talk to coaches, training staff, and select students. How affordable are their sportswear? Are they durable? Do they have problems with shipping or delivery? How often do they have to replace their apparel?

Asking questions of this nature will let you know how business-ey your idea is. It will also help you determine how to source merchandize, set pricing, and retain your customers.

Find a Manufacturer or Supplier

Finding the right manufacturer is the most feasible way to guarantee business growth, but it could also be the most challenging, especially for novice entrepreneurs. It could take time before they get the perfect picture of what you want. You also have to establish communication patterns. Are they responsive? Are they open to feedback? Keep in mind that your customers interact with you, not with your manufacturers or suppliers. You must be confident that your chosen source will not disappoint whenever you call on them to deliver products.

An alternative may be to create your products yourself, though this may be difficult if you aren't venturing into handmade products. Admittedly, it's easier to batch-produce antiseptic hand-wash than make organic skincare products.

CREATE A BRAND NAME OR IDENTITY.

Like Brian Chesky with Airbnb and Morgan Newman with MixedMatch, a brand name marks your brand as unique, and different from other e-commerce stores. But don't fuss about it if you can't find a perfect name. Snapchat didn't come on the first try, and neither did Facebook, Pinterest, or hundreds of other household businesses you know.

If you've defined your industry, look at other businesses within that industry. Compare their names, and check for patterns or similarities. Also, check to see that your name aligns with your industry. *Vibezz* could work for a business in the entertainment space, but it's a no-no for an e-commerce store dealing with electronic gadgets.

Lastly, are your proposed brand name's domain names and social media handles still available? If not, you may have to tweak the name before launching.

Create Your E-commerce Website or Selling Channel.

Owning a website may not be a priority if you're starting out. It's okay to desire a .com domain, like Amazon or Alibaba, but what if you're on a tight budget? What are your alternatives?

Shopify is a splendid choice for e-commerce owners who lack the technical know-how to build a website and the resources to hire a website developer. With various themes, you can easily personalize your online store, using plug-ins like Nudgify and LemonStand. Wix, WordPress, and WooCommerce are other website creation platforms you can explore to get your website running.

Here's also where you introduce your logo, if you have it ready. You can easily adopt a wordmark logo (top brands like Google, FedEx, Etsy, Stripe use wordmark logos).

BUILD A SOCIAL MEDIA PRESENCE.

In chapter three, we covered the essence of creating a vibrant social media presence through consistent content creation, engaging your customers, running social media ads, and tracking the performances of the content you put out.

Your brand name and identity stick in the memory of your target audience when they trust that you consistently turn up on your social media platforms. The catch is, you don't have to be everywhere or use every platform. A skincare brand may find Instagram and TikTok more appealing than Facebook or Twitter, while a brand that sells electronic gadgets prefers YouTube for long-form videos.

You can use your social media platforms to create product listings, including product descriptions and price tags. This simplifies your customers' shopping experience on your channels.

Prepare Your Shipping and Delivery Strategy.

Before you launch, plan your shipping process. If the items in your store are fragile or perishable, you want to plan and cover all delivery as soon as possible. If you sell similar items, you can handle order processing and shipping in-house, working with dispatch companies.

The kind of products you offer will influence your shipping strategy. For instance, you can consider a partnership with a shipping company that delivers nationwide. Research multiple companies, check reviews, and speak with fellow e-commerce owners to know who they use before deciding on an option. While cost conservation is necessary, you must prioritize effectiveness and efficiency over cheap but lacklustre. Your shipping agency may not be the cheapest if they guarantee a great user experience.

Cover the Marketing End

This builds on what you do through your social media channels. As a new e-commerce entrepreneur, you should invest resources in offering your early customers a great shopping encounter. However, when you scale, you can leverage influencer marketing or a Facebook ad campaign to put your products before more users likely to convert to paying clients.

Track your paid campaigns (recall cash outflow?), so you can monitor and compare expenses against revenue and determine the origin of your orders and sales.

DON'T WAIT until everything is perfect before launching. You may need to revisit your launching process often and make necessary adjustments. Test multiple routes (A/B testing) before settling on a plan. Be willing to try again, invest in your e-commerce business, and show up often for your audience.

WORKING **It Out**

1. At what stage would you consider influencer marketing as the next step to growing your business? Why?
2. Do you use a website for your e-commerce business? What three benefits have you enjoyed from using a website?

5

AUDIENCE NURTURING: THE ULTIMATE GAME OF LOVE AND STRATEGY IN SOCIAL MEDIA

WHO IS YOUR BEST FRIEND? You have one, right? Good. Now, think back to the time before you met your best friend for the first time. Let me hazard a guess: they were non-existent to you. Now, think about all that has transpired between you since the first time you met until you became best of friends. A lot, right? The relationship you have with your best friend is similar to the one you want to build with your audience. Just as you cultivate your relationship with your best friend, you must cultivate one with your audience for your business to stand any chance of success.

Much more than anything or anyone, your audience is essential to your entire journey in the world of business. Everything else, your product, its price, your advertising channels and prices, depends on the nature of your audience, and without them, you can build no business. For this reason, most businesses commit time and other resources to develop and maintain an audience base that can consistently churn out customers whose patronage can keep the business afloat as long as possible.

In this chapter, we will explain the concept of an audience in business, explain how you can identify your audience, highlight several strategies you can employ to nurture one for your business and discuss the role that social media can play in this process.

Image Source: DG Studio.

Who is Your Audience?

Your audience is the people most likely to need or desire your product or service. These groups often share attributes like age, gender, education, income, location, and interests.

What does this definition imply? It implies that your product or service determines the people who fall into your target audience. Only medical professionals and healthcare workers will make up your audience if your business sells medical equipment. Even at that, some medical equipment can only be purchased by governments and large health organisations. If your business sells that, then your target audience is even smaller.

Why Knowing Your Audience Matters

Every business exists to serve certain people or organisations. Not knowing who those people or organisations are is a recipe for failure. Understanding your target audience is crucial for one major reason: reducing waste. You're more likely to waste resources if you don't know your target audience. You could create products or services that no one wants to buy. You could also spend money advertising to people who don't need your products/services. This wastage cuts into the soul of your business: profit. A business that can't make a profit consistently is as good as dead.

Getting to Know Your Target Audience

If you did solid market research, you should have a basic idea of the attributes of your business's target audience. To understand them deeper, however, you should find answers to the following questions:

1. Who are they?
2. What are their biggest problems and/or desires?
3. What content do they consume?
4. Where do they hang out?

The first question typically seeks demographic attributes distinguishing them from other consumer groups. The second helps you understand how your business solves these problems or desires. Understanding the content they consume shows you what themes and subjects interest them while knowing where they hang out (online or offline) helps you identify optimal channels for your marketing efforts.

Audience Nurturing: The Only Strategy That Counts

The essence of understanding your audience is to know how best you can cultivate a relationship with them. Remember how you had to learn your friend's likes and dislikes while building your relationship? It's basically the same thing at work here.

Now that you have a better understanding of your audience, nurturing that audience boils down to only one thing: communication. Just like effective communication is the lifeblood of any relationship, it is also the lifeblood of your business. Establishing and maintaining effective communication lines between your business and its target audience is the only way to nurture your audience. Therefore, you must develop a communication plan, that takes your audience from the point of first contact with your business to becoming paying customers or taking any other action you want them to take. Your plan may include any or all of the following:

One-on-one Interactions

Having one-on-one interactions with your target audience can be an effective way to establish and maintain connections with them because of the personal touch that they bring to the relationship. These interactions do not have to be in person, thanks to social media. Also, consider adding personal touches to other communication channels (emails, for example) with your audience, when possible.

Content Marketing

Content marketing is creating and sharing relevant articles, videos, podcasts, and other content to attract engage and retain your audience. It is a long-term approach to marketing capable of yielding enormous results. Major brands, including Hubspot, Buffer, Rolex and LinkedIn, are good examples of developing a robust content marketing strategy to build a formidable brand. The most important thing to note is that the content you create must speak directly to your audience and take the form that best resonates with them.

Social Media: a Magic Toolbox

Social media refers to a number of websites and applications that allows users to create and share information and ideas within a virtual community. These websites and applications, which come in different formats and serve many purposes, have become an essential tool for marketers, salespeople and businesses.

Most social media platforms available fall into the following categories:

- Traditional social networking sites (think Facebook, Twitter, LinkedIn),
- Social review sites (like Yelp and TripAdvisor),

- Image and video-sharing sites (Instagram, Imgur and Snapchat),
- Video hosting sites (Youtube and Vimeo),
- Community blogs (Medium and Tumblr),
- Discussion sites (like Reddit and Quora) or
- Sharing economy networks (like Airbnb and Rover)

These social media platforms offer unique opportunities to relate with your target audience, which you can capitalise on to push your products and services.

Making Magic with Social Media

So how can you use social media to achieve your business goals? Here is a step-by-step approach that you can take:

Be Strategic

This involves developing a plan that will guide your activities on social media. Your strategy should outline your goals for each period and the indicators to look out for when measuring your performance. In developing this strategy, consider your target audience and the resources available. You can also include a publishing plan based on the platforms you have chosen to build on.

Listen and Engage

The opportunity to collect feedback from your audience is of the most essential advantages of social media. This feedback can help you see from your audience's perspective, giving you insights that can help you better serve them.

Analyze

This involves keeping close tabs on how you're faring on social media platforms. Take note of what works and what needs tweaking to perform better.

Working it Out

1. Respond to the four questions in the section on getting to know your audience.
2. Write out every possible means you can use to open and maintain a line of communication with your audience.
3. Identify the social media platforms best suited to nurturing your audience and develop a strategy for using them.

6

BUILD AUTHORITY AND BE THE GO-TO BRAND

WHEN I NEEDED a new laptop sometime last year, I asked a friend (let's call him Jake) for advice. Even though I was not a novice in computer matters at the time, I knew he was vaster in his knowledge and could help me make an excellent choice. I was right - the laptop I eventually purchased was a dream!

If you think long and hard enough, I'm sure you, too, will remember a few occasions in the past when you specifically sought someone out for help, guidance or advice because you believed they had the required knowledge, experience, and expertise to help you at that moment. That is what authority looks like, even in business. Imagine my friend runs a business selling computers and shares the same computer-related information he had shared with me over time with his audience. Many people would have gone to him for advice the same way I did, which would have translated into many more sales for him. That's what authority is about.

In this chapter, we will zoom in on how you can build authority for your brand and command the attention of your target audience. Let's get started.

Let's Define Authority

In simple words, authority is about how your audience sees you. It is the tendency for your prospective customers to view your brand as credible and to take your brand's views or messages as final. As a growing company, you want your audience to see you as dependable, a brand they can rely on. With a high level of authority, your company will have your audience's trust, and a good reputation and can command great influence in your industry, which can be a solid foundation for your business to thrive.

Why Build Authority and How to Do it Right.

As noted earlier, authority is about perception – how others see you. And just as we can contribute significantly in determining how others see us, a brand can do the same. There are numerous pointers on how to build authority in your niche out there, but they all boil down to one simple idea: sharing.

Let's go back to my example in the introduction for a moment. Why do you think I've come to take Jake as an authority in computer matters to the extent that I trusted him to lead me in choosing my next laptop? It's because we have had numerous conversations over time during which he shared his knowledge with me. In addition, I have seen him make great choices when purchasing gadgets for himself and others in the past. That's why I went to him when I had to make a choice. And guess what. I referred her to him the last time someone asked for my guidance in choosing a laptop. If Jake were a business, he'd command significant authority in his market.

Share! Share!! Share!!!

It's important that we focus on the sharing aspect because it is the only thing that matters when it comes to building authority in your industry. Imagine that Jake never shared his knowledge of computer gadgets with me. Even if he were the smartest computer geek in the world, I wouldn't know it. Hence, I wouldn't go to him for help/advice.

Sharing is the most significant way to build a reputation that gives you a continuous advantage in your industry. The advantage is continuous because it usually takes a major upheaval for someone to change their mind once they decide they can trust you. And they are more likely to patronise your business for as long as you keep that trust.

Thankfully, you can share quite a few things as a brand to earn your audience's trust. Let's take a look at some of them.

What To Share And How

Most things a brand can share in building industry authority fall under the following three categories:

· Knowledge and Expertise

· Activities/Processes

· Social Proof (Expert, Celebrity, User)

Knowledge and Expertise

One of the most viable means of earning your audience's trust is to demonstrate appreciable knowledge of your craft and the industry. When people see you or your brand as knowledgeable, they are more likely to stay connected with you and even defer to you when making decisions. You can share your knowledge through several means/channels, including the following:

· Blogging

· Podcasting

· Social media

· Newsletters

· Reports

· E-books, etc.

While each channel has its strengths, finding a perfect blend for your brand is ideal.

Activities/Processes

Have you made some changes in your work processes? Did you purchase a new piece of equipment? Did you attend an A-list conference in your industry? Are you funding a non-profit organisation?

All these activities and more can be a good tool to help your audience see you in a positive light if only you share them.

Social Proof

Although many of us may be unaware, what others think about something or someone often influences how we see them. Social proof refers to what others who have previously connected with your business say about you. These could be users (customers), celebrities or experts in your industry. If any of these people have said something positive about your business, ensure your audience knows. Shout it from the rooftops. It will nurture your reputation and bolster your authority.

More Tips for Building Authority

The following tips can help fine-tune your sharing processes as you build authority for your brand:

- **Stay within your niche.** Your brand exists to serve a particular niche. Ensure all you share is relevant to that niche.
- **Ensure quality.** Your audience sees whatever you share with them as a representation of you. For

example, low-quality images and shallow blog posts riddled with errors will not bode well for your brand.

- **Be consistent.** Showing up always tells your audience they can depend on you.
- **Form beneficial associations.** Associating with other trusted brands in your industry can help improve your brand's authority.
- **Use multiple media.** Sharing across multiple media platforms and using multiple formats (text, images, video) can help maximise your efforts.

Working it Out

1. Identify three brands/individuals you consider authorities in your niche. Find out if there are any similarities in their approaches to sharing with their audience.
2. What have you done before now to build your brand's reputation? What actionable steps can you take going forward?

7

SELL LIKE CRAZY: DON'T JUST TALK A BIG GAME

IF YOU KNOW anything at all as an entrepreneur, you would know that no business can thrive without making sales. Yet, many budding entrepreneurs give very little thought to what their selling process would be like when they start out. Some experienced business leaders have the same faulty line of thought. They think the sales process and all the decisions related to it should be left at the doorstep of the sales team. Such leaders often pay handsomely for that faulty belief. That's why I am devoting this chapter to talking about sales.

Generally speaking, everything we have talked about so far in this book is designed to position your business to generate sales seamlessly. Now, we will zero in on the sales process to gain a deeper understanding that you can apply to your business.

The Sales Process

Every business needs to sell its products or services. To make selling easy, businesses often design a series of repeatable steps that anyone trying to make a sale for the business can take to attract potential customers and convert them into paying customers. Those repeatable steps are what we call the sales process.

With an effective sales process, a business can give its potential customers consistent positive experiences and ensure more of them end up making a purchase. While sales processes may differ slightly, depending on the business, the following are the basic steps a sales process should have:

- Prospecting involves attracting people or organisations who have the potential to become your customers. A potential customer typically needs your product or service and can afford to pay for it.
- Preparation is when you get ready to make the first contact with a potential customer by collecting relevant data about the customer and determining how your product or service can solve their problems.
- The approach is the stage you make the initial contact with your client.

- Presentation is where you demonstrate actively how your product is useful to the potential customer.
- Handling objections is how you address your prospects' concerns, reassuring them that they can move on with the purchase.
- Closing is the stage where you make the sale.
- Follow-up, the final stage, involves staying in touch with the customer after making the sale.

It is important to note that this process is not static. Sometimes two or three stages will happen in quick succession or even simultaneously. Every sale you make follows this process in one way or the other. For online businesses, however, this process has been streamlined into what is called a sales funnel.

The Sales Funnel: Understanding The Customer's Journey

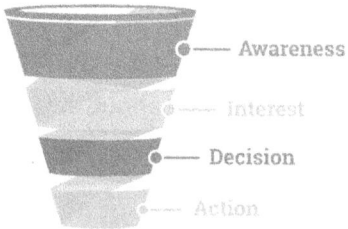

Understanding the sales funnel is essential if you want to

become an exceptional salesperson. A sales funnel describes the customers' journey from awareness to action. It adopts the term funnel because only a small percentage of prospects who arrive at the awareness stage eventually make it to the action stage.

The sales funnel consists of four stages as seen in the illustration above: Awareness, Interest, Desire, and Action. All of your customers will go through these stages. Customers at each stage of the funnel require specific action from a business so that they can move to the next stage.

If well implemented, a sales funnel can help you

- Attract the right audience,
- Qualify the audience to determine those who can and are ready to make a purchase,
- Monitor and track your sales process, and
- Focus your marketing efforts on maximum returns.

How to Build a Sales Funnel

You can build an effective sales funnel by taking the following steps.

Analyze

An analysis of the behavior of your target audience is the first step towards designing a sales funnel that converts. This analysis should focus on identifying your ideal customer and how they are most likely to come across your product. The result of this analysis is essential for the next stage.

Attract

This is where you design something that can attract your potential customers into the funnel. The effectiveness of your funnel rests on getting this stage right, which is why the previous stage is important. Your analysis should reveal what you can use to attract people to your funnel. You can offer something in exchange for the prospects' email addresses. This can be anything from a downloadable resource that offers more detail about the subject of the page they landed on to a free tool or even relevant website content.

Nurture

Now that you have your prospects' email addresses, you can work on convincing them that they need more than the free resource that brought them into your sales funnel. You can send them content that demonstrates how your products can solve a problem for them or meet a need. Many marketing automation tools can help you with this.

Convert

This is where you help the prospect over the last hurdle in the customer journey. You can do this by designing compelling sales pages and FAQs and sharing the link in your messages with prospects.

A Sales Funnel At Work: The Moz Example

At the top of Moz's sales funnels are high-ranking blog

posts on various marketing and related topics relevant to businesses. These blog posts bring visitors to the company's website, where various lead magnets await them. These magnets include free tools, webinars on SEO, white papers and a free software trial.

Whenever a user signs up for any of the lead magnets, they get automated emails encouraging them to take the offer of a free 30-day free trial of the full software.

To access the free trial, users must provide industry and company information, which Moz then uses to customize their correspondence. A sales rep also onboard the prospect, getting more details about their needs in the process.

At the final stage, the sales teams try to address whatever concerns the prospects may still have to help them make the purchase decision.

Working it Out

1. Using the four-step funnel-building process and data you've collected from your audience in previous lessons, map out what you think can be an effective sales funnel for your business.

8

LOYALTY, REFERRALS, AND A
FEEDBACK LOOP YOU CAN'T IGNORE

LET'S start with some statistics.

- It is 5 to 25 times more expensive to acquire new customers than to retain existing ones (Harvard Business Review).
- You are more likely (60-70%) to sell a new product to an existing customer than to new prospects (Hubspot).
- 57% of consumers spend more on brands they are loyal to (Accenture).

This is the bottom line: winning new customers is not enough; you have to find a way to keep them. That's the only way you can build a successful business. In this chapter, we will discuss the feedback loop as a tool for building brand loyalty and ultimately generating more sales for your business. Let's start by defining loyalty.

What is Loyalty?

In lay terms, loyalty refers to the feeling of or act of giving support or allegiance to a person or organization. This definition is also true in marketing parlance. Businesses that serve their customers right often get customers to feel loyal to them. Such customers will continue to patronize the same business over and over even though other businesses offer the same products or services. These customers often associate positive feelings with the business. This, in marketing, is called brand loyalty.

A good example of how this plays out is in people's choice of drink between global brands Coca-cola and Pepsi. Many people around the world will always choose one over the other.

Image source: Strike Social.

Why Should You Care About Brand Loyalty?

The answer is simple: profitability. As the statistics in the introduction to this chapter show, cultivating a group of consumers loyal to your brand can be a sure way to increase your profits. This is so because, with this group, you spend significantly less to make sales as opposed to scouting new customers.

Another fact that should interest you is that these loyalists are not deterred by the price. A good example of that would be Apple. Although Apple's products are amongst the most expensive in the market, the customers consistently align with them, even where there are multiple less expensive options.

How to Build Brand Loyalty

Brand loyalty is about perception. Building it requires fostering a positive perception of your business and you can do that through any of the following ways:

Quality Service Delivery

Providing qualitative service is the single most important thing you can do to build a solid foundation for your business's reputation. And the good thing is that it doesn't have to cost you extra in expenditure. Even if you can devote the biggest budget to marketing, shoddy service delivery or low-quality products will cost you, customers.

Great Customer Service

While providing exceptional customer service can slightly increase your expenditure, that extra investment can yield great results with brand loyalty. Services like 24/7 support, phone operators, and chat reps can make your customers feel valued and encourage them to stay with you.

Loyalty Programmes

A loyalty programme rewards existing customers for patronising your business. This also can be expensive, but the reward is well worth the investment, especially for pricey brands.

Online Community

An online community is another way you can turn your customers into loyalists. Such communities allow you to build meaningful more personal connections with your customers which can increase your value in their estimation.

Referrals

Have you ever been so excited about the service you received from a business that you couldn't keep it to yourself? Enough that you recommended the service to your friends? That's what referrals are.

A referral occurs when an existing customer recommends your business to a new prospect. A business that gets this to happen organically has hit a goldmine.

Referrals are natural offshoots of brand loyalty. Think about how many Apple customers want all their friends to use Apple products.

What is a Feedback Loop?

A feedback loop involves gathering client feedback and using it to improve products continuously. In other words, you review customer feedback, identify patterns and customer pain points, and then choose the most effective way to address those issues.

A feedback loop is essential for several reasons. First, you can use the feedback to keep improving your product to maintain its relevance to the user. Given the constantly changing nature of our world, a product that is a perfect fit now can quickly become obsolete. Getting feedback will help you see when your customer's needs are evolving. Second, a feedback loop can help your customers feel valued and subsequently increase their satisfaction with your product. The third reason is an inevitable outcome of the first two: loyalty and referrals.

How to Create a Feedback Loop

You can create a feedback loop for your business in three easy steps:

1. **Collect Feedback:** The first step in creating a feedback loop is to collect feedback from your customers. Surveys, social listening and live chats are some of the methods you can use to collect this feedback although surveys are ideal for getting structured and detailed responses. You can also use the survey to probe specific issues like why the cart's abandon rate is high.

2. **Analyze Collected Data:** This is where you review the data you've collected to determine what your customers are trying to communicate to you. The data should give you a sense of how

they feel about your product/service and the changes they would like to see.

3. **Close the Loop:** This is where you take action based on the results of your analysis in the second step. Fix bugs that are causing issues, and include new features in response to requests from the feedback. Also, ensure that you inform your customers of the changes you've implemented.

Remember that you have to repeat this process constantly. That's why it's called a loop: it goes on and on. Monitoring the pulse of your customers this way can increase your chances of satisfying them and help you stay ahead in the market.

Working It Out

1. Write down one brand you're loyal to. Now, think about what that brand may have done to make you loyal to it.

2. Which of that brand's activities can you adopt for your business? What other things can you do to build loyalty for your brand?

9

BASICS OF PAID ADVERTISING

FOR THE LAST FEW CHAPTERS, we have focused on getting word about your business out to people who are the most likely to pay for your products or services. Most of the processes we have described depend on the organic flow of messages across online platforms. While those are veritable means of marketing your businesses, they can be limited in their reach and take a long time to yield results.

Paid advertising is an option that can help you extend the reach of your organic efforts and give you results in the short term. In this chapter, we take a quick look at paid advertising and why you should include it in your marketing plan.

What is Paid Advertising?

Paid advertising is a type of advertising that requires an advertiser to pay a fee to a publisher in exchange for the opportunity to display an advertisement to the public. An advertiser here refers to a person or organization who wants to call the attention of the public to a product or service they have for sale.

Paid advertising seeks to reach a target audience and get them to take a specific, predetermined action.

Why Consider Paid Advertising?

As stated earlier, organic marketing efforts can be limited in their reach and take a long time to gain traction. Paid advertising can make up for these limitations and make your marketing more effective. The following are the specific benefits that paid advertising has to offer:

Wider Reach

Unlike organic or owned media advertising which circulates only within your network, paid advertising gives you access to a broader audience base, depending on your business needs. If you are actively seeking new customers, you can increase your chances of success by getting your marketing messages across through paid advertising to new people who are not in your circle.

Audience targeting

Paid advertising also allows you to reach out to specific segments of an audience based on shared interests of similar features. This is great because it allows you to customize your message for each group, increasing its effectiveness. Also, it helps you save money as you can choose to advertise only to a portion of the audience.

Message Testing

Paid advertising also allows you to create different versions of the same advert and test them to see how the audience responds to the messages. This can help to determine what changes to make to your messaging to increase its effect.

Audience Insights

Most paid advertising platforms also offer insights into the characteristics and interests of your audience. These insights can deepen your knowledge of your consumers and help point your marketing efforts in the right direction.

Retargeting

This helps advertisers to target their messages to a user based on their previous online behavior. For instance, if a user lands on your page for the first time and leaves without paid advertising. You can advertise your website to them even when they are on other sites. This can help your business stay on top of mind and increase your chances of converting them.

Quicker Response

With paid advertising, you can get quick results as opposed to organic advertising. Using paid advertising while building your organic reach is therefore a smart move that can yield good returns.

Types of Paid Advertising

Following are the different types of paid advertisements you can use to boost your marketing efforts.

Display Ads

These are online advertisements that use copy, visual elements and a CTA to pass an advertiser's message. They often appear on websites and mobile applications and can give you targeted exposure on the internet. Display advertising typically runs on a cost-per-click (CPC) model, which allows you to pay only when a user clicks on your ad.

Social Media Advertising

All social media platforms offer paid advertising solutions to advertisers who want to reach audiences on their platforms. The most popular are LinkedIn, Facebook, Twitter, Instagram, etc. This type of advertising is one of the most popular because of its effectiveness.

Advertising on social media can help you reach new audiences without significant advertising spend. The major decision you have to make when using social media ads is the choice of platform and this will depend on the audience you're trying to reach. LinkedIn, for instance, is the most ideal for reaching business-to-business audiences.

Pay-per-click

This paid advertising model allows you to pay only when a user clicks on your advert. Search engine advertising is one of the most popular forms of this type of ad and it lets you target consumers who are actively seeking information related to your product or service.

Video Ads

Video advertising has grown significantly in recent times

with the increasing volume of video content available online. Video streaming platforms like Vimeo and YouTube are options to consider for this.

Which Paid Advertising Method is Best?

There is no one best method of paid advertising to use as a business owner. As has been pointed out earlier, the method you choose depends largely on your goals, the audience you're trying to reach and your budget. If you're working with a tight budget, social media advertising is one of the cheapest options available to you, and with the different options available, you are sure to find one that helps you reach your audience.

An ideal situation, however, would be to find the right mix of the various types that can help you achieve your set goals. With social media, you can reach new audiences. With display ads, you can retarget users who have been to your platform before. So, look at your marketing goals before deciding on the type of paid advertising that can best help you achieve them.

Working it Out

1. Based on your understanding of your target audience, specify the online paid advertising methods you think will work best for you.

ABOUT THE AUTHOR

Danny Din is the founder and CEO of a tech company that focuses on developing and creating innovative technological solutions. A creative problem solver, he has helped several entrepreneurs and businesses navigate business development as a consultant and adviser, and he holds patents for his inventions.

Asides from his business advisory roles, Danny's vast experience in the business world is fueled by his time serving on the board of businesses over the last decade. With the wisdom he has gathered from these experiences and insights collated from his devotion to extensive research, Danny delivers insightful speeches on business-related topics to audiences across the country.

He holds Master's and Bachelor's degrees in Aviation Science, Economics, and Business Management, respectively. He also completed an international MBA program, which included training at the Microsoft Ventures Academy.

Before starting his company, Danny served as a drone pilot in the {United States} Air Force, where he rose to the rank of captain and mission commander, successfully leading several missions over a decade.